THE ODD LAST THING
SHE DID

THE ODD LAST THING

SHE DID

P O E M S   B Y

BRAD LEITHAUSER

ALFRED A. KNOPF   NEW YORK   1998

THIS IS A BORZOI BOOK
PUBLISHED BY ALFRED A. KNOPF, INC.

Copyright © 1998 by Brad Leithauser
All rights reserved under International and Pan-American Copyright Conventions.
Published in the United States by Alfred A. Knopf, Inc., New York, and simultaneously
in Canada by Random House of Canada Limited, Toronto.
Distributed by Random House, Inc., New York.
www.randomhouse.com

Library of Congress Cataloging-in-Publication Data
Leithauser, Brad.
The odd last thing she did : poems / by Brad Leithauser. — 1st ed.
p.   cm.
ISBN 0-375-40141-5
I. Title.
PS3562.E4623033   1998
811'.54—dc21   98-14565
                                CIP

Manufactured in the United States of America
First Edition

AUTHOR'S NOTE

In the eight years since my last book of poems, I seem to have accumulated various debts, some of which I hope to discharge here. Many of these poems first appeared in magazines: "A Honeymoon Conception," "Plus the Fact of You," "Small Waterfall," "A False Spring," and part of "Triptych: A Marsh in March" in *The New Yorker;* "The Odd Last Thing She Did," "At an Island Farm," "Play," "Blessing for Malcolm Lowry," and "Shiloh, 1993" in *Poetry;* "Set in Stone," "Yet Not Yet," and "The White Jet" in *Adelaide Review;* "Another Dream" and "Later" in *The London Review of Books;* "Red Leather Jacket" and "A Flight Up the Coast" in *The Atlantic Monthly;* "After the Detonation of the Moon" in *The New York Review of Books.* I thank the poetry editors of these publications.

And I need to thank assorted friends and family, living and deceased. "A Honeymoon Conception" and "1944: Purple Heart" are dedicated to my mother, Gladys Garner Leithauser; "The Odd Last Thing She Did" to Brock Walsh and Joy Horowitz; "At an Island Farm" to Sigurdur Tomasson and Steinunn Bergsteinsdottir, at whose summer house it was written; "Red Leather Jacket," "Plus the Fact of You" and "Small Waterfall" to Mary Jo Salter; "Triptych: A Marsh in March" to Peter Kane Dufault; "After the Detonation of the Moon" to Peter Davison; "Cat and Mustang: A Still Life" to Joe Phillips; "Play" to Peggy O'Shea; "Clouds in Winter: Dusk" to Emily Lodge and Robert Pingeon; "A Flight up the Coast" to Arthur Higbee; "The White Jet" to Mary Jarrell; "Answer to a Child's Question" to the Garners, William, Wendy, Elizabeth, and Hannah; "The Visa" to Jacques Bonnet; and "An Old Hunter" and "Crest and Carpet" to the memory of my father, Harold Edward Leithauser.

FOR RICHARD LYON

sometime roommate

&

full-time soulmate

CONTENTS

I   MEN AND WOMEN

II STONES TREES BREEZES STARS

III MEN AND MEN

I MEN AND WOMEN

A HONEYMOON CONCEPTION (1952)

All night, though not a flake fell, the snow deepened . . .
From Grand Central their train joggled forth (stray
     snow scraps wadded in gulleys, like
a leafletting not fully swept away)
at dusk; in Connecticut, the darkness opened

(but here and there, a street lamp's sliding glow
showed how the scraps had formed a quilt), as they
     toasted themselves in the dining car,
their glances, given the press of what still lay
before them, sometimes shying toward the window.

In Vermont (though in the sleeping car they kept
the shade drawn and so never saw the play
     of bridal white on white on white,
dark pine fastnesses suddenly giving way
to snow-packed moon-limned stands of birch), they slept,

part of the time. But neither one had ever
been wider awake than on the following day,
     in Quebec, Canada (a city
of foreign signs—*gare, rue, petit déjeuner*—
and everything wrapped in white except the river,

whose fierce black urgings made of the whole place
a kind of high-piled dockyard, every slipway
     loaded with crates of lace and crystal).
On a noon walk, happily mapless, they
chanced a side street and soon came face to face

with a colossal, larger-than-life snowman
in red scarf and blue cape, who, in his warm,
     generous, featureless way, smiled
blessings upon them. (Or snow*woman*?—it was a form
smooth and rich-bellied, as if big with child.)

ANOTHER COUPLE

She wanted things respectable,
and even in derangement meant to keep them so.
    She'd been a widow thirty years,
    overseeing her eighties with a noble
dignity, when her mind started to go;
      and when, moved to a home, she met
a man who lit a sort of seasoned flame
    within, she quickly let him know
his place. She called him John, her husband's name—
    for she was faithful even yet.

This John of hers was no less gone,
though his gaze flared with a fierce, guileful clarity
    the day he pressed me to his side
    and said—addressing not her grandson
but a young fella on the make—"She's screwy
    upstairs, mm? Got the whole thing wrong.
Calls me Johnny—I'm Jack—and likes to think
    we're married. What a load of hooey.
Women . . ." he marvelled, adding, with a wink,
    "You learn how to string them along."

Of legendary littleness,
　　at least in family circles, was the stone
　in Aunt Yvonne's engagement ring. And she knew,
　　　in her arch way, how to expand upon
　　　　such smallness: What's this? Why, no less
　　a natural marvel than her very own
　　　　　Canardley Diamond. (You
　can 'ardly see the thing.) Her needle-point.
　　　　　Her half-a-glint.

That's all Frank could afford, she would
　　cry merrily—as poor as that, back then!
. . . Yet a gem of sufficient size to see her through
　　　not only forty years of marriage
　　　　but nineteen more of widowhood,
　including that last, seated decade when
　　　　the vast white shadows threw
　a mist on any world that might contain
　　　　a thing so fine.

Something of a surprise
To find her set in black and white,
Although she was, given the portrait's date,
Bound to be. *Red,* I remembered her dress
As *red*—all the more puzzling since
I had so many details right: the out-thrust
Chin (and hip), the healthy bust,
The fervent, faintly cross-eyed glance,
The grand masses of upswept hair,
The hand gracefully but securely placed
Upon the shoulder of the girl in the chair
Beside her, who gazes up with—constancy?
More than that: the humble-faced
Complaisance of the lifelong devotee.

The portrait has a clean-
Angled precision life too seldom shows,
Their branching futures written in their pose:
Clearly, the pigtailed younger one
(My grandmother Cassie) will embrace
As her soul's task the role of the Good Sister,
Who would in every crisis minister
To the other, the Bad One, whose gaze says *Yes,*
I'll be there when my ship arrives!
The Good looks up; the Bad, out and away.
The one is other-, the other self-directed.
What's left them purely is the day-by-day
Embodying of the paired, divergent lives
They have, so early on, elected.

The year's 1916
And the older girl—no girl, she's twenty-three—
Soon will leave Gorvin, Tennessee,
Her home and family, for Washington,
Our nation's capital. She's out to seize
The day, the ring, the prize. The portrait's a farewell.
A *Watch me go.* Or a *Damn-them-all-to-hell.*
Yet who'd deny her her opportunities?
Clearly, she's far too smart, too lovely, too
Lively a blend of fairy-tale princess
And modern girl for Gorvin to possess
Her in the end. Winch up the castle gates.
A bright new roadster's coming through.
Destiny 'phones. Another world awaits.

What awaits presently
Is a William (Billy) Wilmot Morton III,
Whom she will meet the very week she's hired
At the Red Cross dispensary.
Whatever can she hope to set beside
His sheepskin (Princeton) on the wall,
Family (Massachusetts bluebloods all),
And rank (Lieutenant)? What can she provide
Fit for a William Wilmot Morton,
Except her mountain-bred mother wit
And the good looks issuing from
Her too-few decent clothes and that proud name
Of hers—Veronica—which she'll permit
No one (dear Billy least of all) to shorten?

Back home in Gorvin, though,
For that young correspondent who's forever
Posting another homespun letter
An old nickname persists: Cass writes to no
Veronica but "Very." The girl's naive
Presumption that her distant, glamorous
Sister would welcome news of various
Boondock-doings, served up with neither verve
Nor irony (such things as, *Herbert Seaver*
Is building a new barn, or *Jim Duke landed*
A six-pound catfish, or *Old Wally Small*
Does not look well, or *Tripps broke his ankle*),
Turns out, surprisingly, to be well founded.
Who would have guessed that Very was a *saver*?

    She saved, naturally,
Her Billy's billets-doux from France. *They sure*
Do welcome us. Like Sherman said, War
Is swell. And: *As for children? Well, we'll see,*
But I do think four has a nice round sound.
And: *Since I was a boy, reading and rereading*
Prescott, I've always dreamed of heading
to Mexico—I think of it as Magic Ground.
Tlaxcala, Cholula, Chapultepec Hill.
Darling, are you game? They say
It's another world. News of his death (Ors, France;
Crossing a canal; machine gun fire; struck once,
In the right temple) failed to reach her until
Two days after Armistice Day.

She fell less splendidly.
Years passed, about which little's known. There were
To be no trips to "other worlds" for her;
She stayed in Washington. In '23,
Aged thirty-one, she married a Tom Kidd,
Who owned a shoe store. As for children? None—
And no Kidd either, four years on:
Divorce, her first of three. "Her whole life would
Have been so different," Grandma one day said,
"Had Billy lived. *They* were ideally matched.
But when he died—" Her features twitched,
As if she'd pricked herself with one
Of her sewing needles. "—she—she came undone."
"How do you mean?" "Well, she was often sad."

—And often soused, I fear,
For it turned out (my mother later imparted
What her own mother'd been too broken-hearted
To tell me) Very liked a glass of beer,
Wine, bourbon, gin. She had her binges;
At times she was "just fine." In '33
She moved up North, to Rock Ridge, Kentucky,
With husband number four, a Mr. Hodges . . .
Or, you might say, with husband number three-
A, since neither church nor state had ever
Blessed her union with this man—
A triggering irregularity
Turned up by Cassie's husband, Trevor.
And so the Civil War began.

10

Trevor the autocrat,
Famed for his ramrod posture, knew no doubt:
As far as the family went, Very was *out*.
Henceforth, no dealings—hear? And that was that.
But visits? his wife begged. None. *Letters?* No.
The bond between the sisters was no more . . .
Well, war is hell and Cassie went to war.
She cut off conversation with *him*—oh,
She'd field a question, with a word or phrase,
But that was all. And so it went for days.
She knew, of course, she was outmanned, but mutely
Maintained her ground; it was a sort of siege.
She watched him reason, threaten, redden, rage,
Slam fists upon the table resolutely . . .

The Fall of Trevor Romer
(Still a starred item in the family annals)
Took thirty days. "Along with everything else,
It was for her an endless source of humor,"
My mother explained. "Each time she'd speak of it
She'd laugh till—literally—the tears ran.
He *cursed* her, Poppa, the world's most proper man . . .
What was so dear, though, was just how unfit
He was for cursing women. Well, you see—"
(Now *her* eyes, too, begin to water,
And in my life I've known no laugh so rich
As this, passed on, mother to daughter,
Intact through half a century)
"He called your grandma a real son of a bitch."

But now retreat somewhat . . .
I'm twelve and visiting Grandma and,
Alone in the guest-bed, close at hand,
Seize on a sin that would no doubt
Shock the old girl out of her skin. Mom, too.
And likewise every female of my acquaintance,
Except perhaps . . . And thus begins my dalliance
With *her*, the nether half, the sister who
(Or so suggests her portrait's steamed
Expression, hip thrust tight against her dress)
Might understand my rapturous distress.
(In fact our union's deeper than I'd dreamed:
The strange truth is I soon do dream
Of her . . . Dream that I'm home, my parents' room,

Yet when I open wide
Their bathroom door, a dark new hall extends.
I walk it *slowly*. Ajar at the end's
A door I open with my knee—inside,
In a hot wash of sun, she's standing. Yes,
Although her back's to me (she's at the window)
There's no mistaking who it is. I *know*,
And when she swings round, in her plush red dress,
Her shoulders are bare and, what's more
In all this heat, they're white as snow. The air's
Ablaze. Her pretty hands are cupped. She peers
At me, declares, *I knew you'd come to me,*
And floats her hands apart. Set free,
Pink petals loop like snowflakes to the floor.)

There was unearthly light
As well—auroral yellows, spacy blues—
On my first night in Vera Cruz.
(I'm twenty-one, it's my first sunset
On foreign soil.) We're eating our way through
A bowl of grapes, at a sidewalk cafe,
Mother and I. "One puzzle piece you may
Not know," she says. "Aunt Very died of—" "Lou
Gehrig's disease." "Yes, which in her case meant
That her coordination slowly went,
Till in the end she couldn't manage locks
And keys, utensils, buttons. It was as if
She was still there but her body'd drifted off."
The spoon in her own hand quakes.

"Before the end she met
A Mr. Stumm, who had a wife . . . (That's just
The start—by all accounts he was a first-
Class bastard.) Big and *mean,* he used to get
In bar-fights and, I gather, sometimes he'd
Hit her—Very—too. Still, he owned a business,
Hardware I think, and paid her bills I guess.
Anyway, though it wasn't contagious, she tried
To keep it from him. The disease.
Afraid he'd leave her. Well!—talk about hell . . .
She should have gone to Momma, but always men
Were who she'd bet on, and now she couldn't tell
Even her lover when the worst blow came down.
D'you see just how un*speak*able it was?"

Not yet, no. Later on,
Though, in my hell-hot hotel room,
I bring her back—the Very of my dream.
Tossing, turning things over, I begin
To gather how it must have been for her.
All the small ruses . . . When he comes
To pay a call, surely she dims
The lights—the better to hide her tremor.
Likewise refrains from picking up
A comb. A plate. A coffee cup.
Get things ready beforehand! Don't
Move much. Stay bright—but what to talk about?
(Each has a job of sorts. His is the rent.
And hers? The same as ever. Putting out.)

I track her to her bed—
Naked, tipsy, the snow of her skin gone sallow,
The once-majestic hair sprawled on her pillow.
The fall of petals has rigidified
To sleet, slamming against the pane.
It's time, and now it's Open wide for him
This body of hers that has become a tomb
Against whose walls he's knocking yet again,
Invoking entry. (Meanwhile, some
Radio romeo's selling songs of love.
Outside, she feels the hick-town streets go numb,
The cold is falling . . .) (Meanwhile, day
By day, the grunted fanfare of
His latest arrival drifts further away.)

1944: PURPLE HEART

"Back—he'd come back, though with a sewed-up chest,
crutches, a leg-cast nearly bigger than

he was, and naturally he's supposed to rest.
Rest? He has to show his girl 'a time,'

out for some splashy meal he can't afford,
and so there we are, he's in uniform and I'm

in a borrowed white silk dress, struggling aboard
a crowded streetcar, and a nice old man

offers up a seat, which, thank you very much,
our soldier accepts—on my behalf. I nearly died.

Sit *in* it? I wanted to crawl *under* it
and not come up, I was so mortified.

I'm eighteen, and healthy—how can I sit
and leave the soldier swaying on his crutch?

*

It was his gallantry is what it was.
Mine would be the first seat had he been well

and was he going to play the slacker just because
one of his knees was peppered with shrapnel?

What could I do? I could have argued across town,
he would never have budged. But when I sat,

the man beside me did—budged—gave up *his* seat.
Only then would our soldier-boy sit down.

It must seem so quaint to you . . . It does to *me,*
and I was there. But things were somehow less—

less absurd, fifty years ago. That's a gallantry
long gone, which is only right"—but not without one

small word of thanks delivered by a son
grateful to have known so choice a foolishness.

What you took away
was something more precious, it turned out,
even than your presence—that of a neat-
knit woman, lined and fine-boned,
 given to lingering at the holiday
  table for hours on end, although
  with little herself to say.

It took us some time—
your death taking us by surprise—
to net our losses. But when questions arose
about some loose scrap of family lore
 (Who was the Austrian martinet
  so strict he wouldn't have his eight-
  year-old son's arm set

when the boy broke it
playing on the banned barn roof? Who
sent the starter's crank winging through
the windshield of his sluggish Model T?
 Who eloped with Phil "the Bill" Hill?
  Who stole his grandma's silver? Whose
  son starved at Andersonville?),

someone would say,
"Edith could have told us that . . ." You
who never married, were never known to
conduct a serious romance, whose
　long career was famously dull
　　(linking names to numbers—directory
　　assistance for Ma Bell),

　and who nowhere seemed
to wring from anyone one single strong
emotion beyond an unthinking
gratitude for your surpassing
　gentleness, managed ultimately,
　　nonetheless, to enlist
　　and mobilize a multi-

　generational
army . . . now lost, the lot of them, all
of them gone! And they went in loyal
silence, theirs being a campaign
　in which, when history's unlikeliest
　　general moved, the troops moved with her:
　　on a night-march into the world's least

　understood terrain.

The last time, ever,
I caught your gaze,
I found—four in the one,
three in the other—a blaze
of seven sparks in your eyes,
and vowed to myself, Here's
the constellation by which
to recollect her always.

Keeping your eyes in mind,
still it took years to see,
oh dearest prime,
that the four and three
matched up—cup and handle—
with the Little Dipper, whose
outmost tip's the lodestar. Even
now I'd have you guiding me.

What made the moment was the lack of all
Premeditation, calculation, talk:
Oh, I was *talking* (what, I can't recall)
Until, look catching look, we slowed our walk,
Stopped still. Right then, now, never having done
Anything on earth like this before, I brought
My face toward yours . . . You had no time for thought.
Instinct alone lifted your mouth to mine.

(The beauty was just this: there was no thinking.
And that I came undone at a mere kiss—
My mind a flood-rush like no flood's before,
Such that no past gasped groping, no headlong sinking
Of flesh in flesh could touch the force of this—
Was a boon, to be sure, but nothing more.)

ANOTHER DREAM

Unreckonable,
the expanses crossed to reach
the dark before this lighted ledge no
deeper than a bookshelf, holding a white beach
with two live finger-puppet figures—but here
you stand, stooping before them, nonetheless.
You've made it; lean closer; and surely, yes,
wafting through these pinpoint ingenuities,
that *is* the smell of brine . . . And how fine the details!
(Even the kelp, long abandoned by the sea
as hopelessly tangled, comes with tiny, tinny flies
among its lichen-like, salt-stain blossoms . . .) She,

wearing nothing,
evidently, under her
powder-blue plastic raincoat,
hunches by a driftwood fire, face so astir
with reflections, one can't help reading there
a crystallizing impulse to be elsewhere. He—well,
he's another matter, isn't he? Truth to tell,
thinking's the furthest thing from his thoughts
as he tilts back on tiptoe till his spine cracks
delightfully, next assesses the ocean, section
by section, with a gaze that says, All this
too, coming my way—isn't it perfection?

A car is idling on the cliff.
Its top is down. Its headlights throw
A faint, bright ghost-shadow glow
On the pale air. On the shore, so far
Below that the waves' push-and-drag
Is dwindled to a hush—a kind
Of oceanic idle—the sea
Among the boulders plays a blind-
Fold game of hide and seek,
Or capture the flag. The flag
Swells and sways. The car
Is empty. A Friday, the first week
Of June. Nineteen fifty-three.

A car's idling on the cliff,
But surely it won't be long before
Somebody stops to investigate
And things begin to happen fast:
Men, troops of men will come,
Arrive with blazing lights, a blast
Of sirens, followed by still more
Men. Though not a soul's in sight,
The peace of the end of the late
Afternoon—the sun down, but enough light
Even so to bathe the heavens from
Horizon to shore in a deep
And delicate blue—will not keep.

Confronted with such an overload
Of questions (most beginning, *Why would she* . . .
So gifted, bright, and only twenty-three),
Attention will come to fix upon
This odd last thing she did: leaving
The car running, the headlights on.
She stopped—it will transpire—to fill
The tank a mere two miles down the road.
(Just sixteen, the kid at the station will
Quote her as saying, "What a pity
You have to work *today*! It's not right . . .
What weather! Goodness, what a night
It'll be!" He'll add: "She sure was pretty.")

Was there a change of plan?
Why the stop for gas? Possibly
She'd not yet made up her mind? Or
Had made it up but not yet settled
On a place? Or could it be she knew
Where she was headed, what she would do—
And wanted to make sure the car ran
For hours afterward? Might the car not be,
Then, a sort of beacon, a lighthouse-
In-reverse, meant to direct one not
Away from but toward the shore
And its broken boulders, there to spot
The bobbing white flag of a blouse?

Her brief note, which will appear
In the local *Leader,* contains a phrase
("She chanted snatches of old lands")
That will muddle the town for three days,
Until a Professor E. H. Wade
Pins it to Ophelia—and reprimands
The police, who, this but goes to show,
Have not the barest knowledge of Shakespeare,
Else would never have misread "lauds"
As "lands." A Detective Gregg Messing
Will answer, tersely, "Afraid
It's not our bailiwick. Missing
Persons, yes; missing poems, no."

(What's truly tragic's never allowed
To stand alone for long, of course.
At each moment there's a crowd
Of clowns pressing in: the booming ass
At every wake who, angling a loud
Necktie in the chip dip,
Airs his problems with intestinal gas,
Or the blow-dried bonehead out to sell
Siding to the grieving mother . . . Well,
Wade sent the *Leader* another *brief word:*
"Decades of service to the Bard now force
Me to amend the girl's little slip.
'Chaunted' not 'chanted' is the preferred . . .")

Yet none of her unshakable entourage
—Pedants, pundits, cops without a clue,
And a yearning young grease monkey—are
Alerted yet. Still the empty car
Idles, idles on the cliff, and night
Isn't falling so much as day
Is floating out to sea . . . Soon, whether
She's found or not, her lights will draw
Moths and tiny dark-winged things that might
Be dirt-clumps, ashes. Come what may,
The night will be lovely, as she foresaw,
The first stars easing through the blue,
Engine and ocean breathing together.

AT AN ISLAND FARM

If only the light might last,
  the mild sea-breeze hold steady,
I think perhaps I could soon be ready
    to relinquish a past

  that let go of *me* as surely
  as some stern wind last year
may have seized a wheat stem by the ear
    and shaken it, purely

  without a thought for
  whether the seeds were drowned
or whether, aloft, some few of them found
    another shore.

The goal I suppose is a steadied mind—
to replace with wood and stone
and insulated wire
what was contrived of flesh and bone,
blood and blood's desire;

isn't the final end to find
that haven where where you are
matters as much to me
as whether or not, on another block,
the wind's now ruffling a tree?

Had I not spoken first
when we met that clouded morning
after a broken night
in which we'd slept apart;

had I not stunned myself
at the start I underwent,
kindling at the sight
of you far across the park

(bright—so bright your jacket's
red on that dark day
whose fallen leaves were drifting
from brown to a final gray);

had I then, possessed by a flame
that stirred up the ashes of
a cool cover of pigeons,
not broken into a run

(past a row of frost-gripped benches
and a low, a wire-caught kite
that hung its head in shame),
and reached you almost breathless;

well, suppose I hadn't spoken
first, dipping my head
toward a spooneristic kiss
from you who glowed as red

as any Queen of Hearts,
hadn't cried, "My dear, you luck
like Lady Look herself!"
would *you* have managed better?

What would you have said?

The sun, having come
down hard all day, goes out softly from
our limbs tonight, the burn we'd otherwise
   be feeling tamed to a banked glow
by one of the white, magic lotions pulled
   from your big black sack of supplies.

   We're both up to the brim—
with rice, little shrimp, red snapper aswim
in a spiced lime-laced broth, greens in a mustard
   vinaigrette, black beans with cilantro
and chilis, pineapple wedges, papaya,
   coffee, some nutmeg-dusted custard.

   And my head's brimming too,
for as I'm drifting off, my back to you,
your breathing seems to flutter through a green
   undergrowth and I'm standing where
this morning we stood, dumbstruck to behold
   more flowers than either'd ever seen

   outside a garden: one
whole hillside under blossom, overrun
as by a river, golds, whites, pinks, reds, fluid
   and aflame!
         (But now my sleep-tilted
task is to compute if blooms outnumber breaths,
or breaths blooms . . . And let's say you take

eight breaths a minute, that's some sixty
minutes per flower and don't forget to carry the one but which
one is it?—and why at night do numbers clamor so, packed
  too tight too are they, no other room
to bloom, carry the one?—carry the sun under your skin,
  we do, and if you add a one to two, too? . . .)

    I arrive at my sum
down at the base of the slope, where I come
upon you, slyly deep in foliage,
  sheltering from the sun,
dipping hot red feet in a bouldered stream,
  three buttons of your blouse undone.

SMALL WATERFALL: A BIRTHDAY POEM

Maybe an engineer,
stumbling on this small, all-
but-forest-swallowed waterfall—
a ten-foot drop at most—
could with some accuracy
say just how much energy
goes unharnessed here.

Enough, is it, to bring light
and heat to the one-room hut one might
build here at its foot—where,
piecing together the *hush*
in the current's *hurl* and *crash,*
a lone man might repair
to fix a shopworn life?

Enough, anyway, to light
one image in my head: this mist-
laced column of water's
as slim as a girl's waist—
yours, say, narrow still despite
the tumble down the birth canal
of a pair of nine-pound daughters.

Well, there's nothing for it but,
sloshing my way across the pool,
I must set whimsy into fact—
which is how, one blazing, cool
August day in New Hampshire, I
come to be standing with my
arms round a cataract.

. . . Nothing new in this, it turns out—
for I know all about embracing
a thing that flows and goes
and stays, self-propelled and -replacing,
which in its roundabout route
carries and throws, carries and throws
off glints at every turn, bringing

all it touches to flower
(witness those flourishing daughters).
  Your reach exceeds my grasp, happily,
for yours is the river's power
to link with liquid, unseen threads
the low, far, moon-moved sea
and the sun's high-lit headwaters.

A FALSE SPRING

(She who'd been taken
hostage—when?—been bound
and drugged, kept in all things
in the dark, now at last found
she'd begun to waken.)

So gently that year did
January come on, it teased
out the crocus, half-hid
in snow, gilded the willows, eased
the forsythia into bloom.

(But a good hard blow
sent her blindly back under.
Escape? A mere dream,
and that the dream came in a glow
of green, of gold, no wonder.)

II   STONES TREES BREEZES STARS

TRIPTYCH: A MARSH IN MARCH

I. Cattails

It's like the morning-after after some
   outré/ultimate year-end blowout,
       and clearly whatever
     cleanup was started was a shall we say
       half-hearted endeavor . . .
Most of the loose-strung bunting's been
taken down, but hasn't yet been swept away,
    the floor's a mess—a massacre—

     of broken-limbed furniture,

shattered glass is everywhere, and wet
   wadded heaps of trampled favors await
      the incinerator.
     Of course every party reaches a close
      sooner or later,
though you'd never know it from those (still
at it—always the last to go) tight-knit politicos,
    murmuring, nodding, prodding at each other

    with their ponderous cigars.

II. Photosynthesis

Fine as the lines bred in the dead of summer
Sealing a fallen damselfly inside
The planar dungeon of a spider's web;
Fine, even, as the plunging comet's tail
Of a transcendental number, its receding
Ever unrepeating line of figures
Vaporing off behind the terminal
Chunk of a decimal point; indeed as fine
As those luminous line-segments by which
Your figure-hungry spirit constellates
The underrepresented heavens . . . just so
Perfectly near to naught's the process whereby
Celestial gold's spun into earthly green:
Even now, even here, light gives way to the weight
Of life, photon to plankton, and so on
Up the out-flung, ply-building chain that yields,
In time, the form-fit emerald lace-mail of
A mallard's head, cracked-whip exactitudes
Of a frog's tongue, incurving white-gold-freaked
Snail's shell's whorlings—creatures all soon to be
At home here.
                    Soon—soon: as the ice relents,
As breezes find, at last, liquids to quiver
(Rustling fresh oxygen into the mud,
Raising rich, dead biota to the surface),
Vascular systems will thaw into use,

Calyces loosen toward a snakelike shucking,
And roots take deeper root. It's nearly time
For that display wherein our branching Plant
Kingdom unveils its thousand thousand-and-one
Ways of performing the same trick: the matter-
Of-fact molecular miracle of turning
Water and carbon dioxide into glucose.

III. General Uprising

Dawn finds them—the living—curled up in
  ditches, tucked into tussocks, soddenly
      outflung on fraying
    mats of leaves, and calls them to rise, somehow
      or other, swaying
on their makeshift canes and crutches . . . How long
it was!—a spell so dark, so chill, it's only now
      there's any telling the numbly

      slumberous from the dead.

They rise up needful, ineffectual. Survival's
  rooted elsewhere. These, they're helplessly
      bound to that golden
    inner circle so far above their mortal share—
      toward whose heedless, unbeholden
extravagances they in their necessitous
tenderness extend the cups, the bare
      plates, the empty, peremptory hands

      of their upstart beggardom.

Yet what do you answer
the voice within that cries
on the first day of a long-delayed spring,
But it all comes too soon!

Before we are ready for
so heady a prize
a thousand icy streets must be paced
under an iced-over moon.

AFTER THE DETONATION OF THE MOON

Hate Winter? Here's a Scientist's
Answer: Blow Up the Moon
Headline, *Wall Street Journal*

We *were* overwhelmed, just as they'd intended:
for wasn't this the greatest show of clout
the world had ever seen, and all without
loss of a single life—an exploit splendid
no less for its humanity than for
its sweeping expertise? And they were right
that life would go on as it had. The night
was still the night. The stars blazed all the more
in a cleared sky.
              These days we seldom fall
for that trick of the eye by which some tall
mist-softened clocktower or fogged street lamp will
recall a changing face, and something tidal
heave in the chest, then ebb, leaving us all
to wonder when if ever this sea too might still.

CAT AND MUSTANG: A STILL LIFE

A big yellow cat that has taken
refuge under the rear
of an old Mustang watches
the boots and umbrellas pass

with such an air of benign
well-being on its features
one might suppose the car
only recently was parked there

and provided in addition
to a dry outlook on the rain
a lingering zone of warmth from
the curl of its tailpipe; what more

could any of us ask than a
flair for improvising
under just such unpromising
vagabond conditions

the distant creature comforts
of that prime weatherproof lair
whose warmth—whose all—was a constant,
and a given, a given good?

PLAY

I

Easily, first our red canoe's
upturned reinforced nose

coasts across the rounded rim
of the bridge's shadow, then a room-

like enclosure's thrown over our shoulders and we're
in on a sort of open-ended show, where,

back and forth on the rusted ceiling,
up-angling sunlight's sailing.

    Yet it's a harbor where, try as we might,
    we can't hold our own, quite,

    and though we paddle backwards, hard
    toward the bow, we're spirited off—yard

    by yard, driven irresistibly along,
    back under the sky. The current's too strong.

II

Even so, we're under long enough to bring the scene
lastingly to life: a zone where the sun,

though splintered, crowns another domed firmament,
this one brown, and the river's roofed voices mount

to a ceaseless, clamorous *hush* . . . a place where
spiders in tatters live out a high-wire

existence, somehow coming to base
their very lives above the onrushing abyss.

    Upon the bridge's underside the broken sun, too,
    throws a web, pliant and vast, and through

    the spider-nets the solar-nets brightly go flying,
    as if to show up the uselessness in anyone's trying

    to snare, however fine the line unwound,
    matters of spirit in the matter-bound.

III

—Or are we, in our rush to extract
lessons from the place, almost tricked

into missing the all-but-unmistakable? Might it not
be play, purely, that slides the one net

inside the other—the selfsame urge that bends
monkey tails into question marks, lends the clownfish bands

of motley, builds, of blackness, the more multi-mooned
of our planets and the see-through micropalace of a diamond?

What but play's at work, when an old bridge (one that must
groan and shudder each time, in a rolling hill of dust,

another flatbed truck comes heavily
rattling over) all the while turns out to be

undergirded by a mesh of wheeling
water-filtered sun across its nether ceiling?

One forgets
> how the clouds there
in the upper atmosphere
> escape our seasonal vagaries,

and if colder
> now than on
the hottest August noon
> it's by a couple of degrees.

Always
> they float within
a zone where the lungs would burn
> and the blood freeze.

Sunlit inlets,
hot blinding gold
scintillations
gliding through tight-
stitched tapestries
of living green;
and skies azure
from one long out-
slung horizon
to the other,
ether without
flaw or tincture,
unshadowed and
unsoundable . . .

One might as well,
on such a day,
call this the Coast
of Anywhere—
some anyplace
plush, sumptuous,
underpeopled:
the jungly rim
of Sumatra
perhaps, the shores
of Honduras,
a littoral
Africa teemed
to the sea's hem.

Underpeopled,
too, our little
twelve-seater, its
three passengers
neatly equal
to the flight crew.
Yes, we're a sort
of family
circle—though one
whose hearth-fire is,
on such a day,
the globe itself—
with something of
a family's

seasoned silence
(years behind us,
years to come). Why
breathe a word? What
experience
can life dispense
more delicious
than to gaze down
from Heaven toward
a world scarcely
recognized—ours
the rare vantage
of creatures both
lost and divine?

The morning's grown so still,
A jetstream spreads upon

The surface of the lake
In consummate detail,

Fanning out behind
Like the trail of a paddling bird.

As it swims across, you find
You're all but able to make

The creature out: rare swan
Of swans, the white jet—

But a ghost-swan that can unveil
A rich billowing wake

And leave the waters unstirred
May be more marvel yet.

Why so dark today? I guess
Because
The light of the sun,
Having commandingly spanned
Some ninety-two million nine hundred and
Fifty thousand miles of icy space,
With but a mile to run
Chanced to meet up with a wall
More delicate than lace,
Feathers, gauze,
Tissue paper;
You see, the torch borne on high for all
Ninety million miles (and change) was—yes—
Quenched by water vapor.

The slipping out
is always so much simpler
than what memory makes of it.
Afterwards, somehow, you forget—

you with all your
sly self-inducements, your ingenious
means of engineering for
yourself one more departure—

just what it's like:
that it flows; comes unprompted;
is gentle (less inclined to knock
down than dissolve the walls); and quick.

Perhaps the vast
sky-sprawl of a small Ruisdael landscape
will do the trick, or Dowland's last
shiver of a bass viol, or just

a spider, green
as the rubber-plant leaf she bridges
in a clean side-sweep of morning sun;
maybe contrails will bring it on,

laid one upon
the other like tinder twigs before
a fiery dusk, or a dusty brown
lock of hair, bound in sky-blue ribbon.

Whatever—here,
now, the moment mounts, and borne aloft or
born again again it comes clear
that no attempts to name it matter . . .

Call it your state
of grace, call it release, oneness,
catharsis, what-have-you—what
matters is that rarely, and yet

reliably,
the process in its course recurs. It
asks patience. In time, you're to be
granted a new exit. And an entry.

TRIPTYCH: TROPICS, PSYCHOTROPICS

... the panther stands by, awaiting the moment when he,
too, can claim his share.
Henri Rousseau, on his painting *The Hungry Lion*

I. Very Hot

It is the sun compels
the plants to launch such cruel postures, pulls
them high into cutthroat distensions, packs them in
in a relentless, thriving confinement ... Think
of the sharp ingenuities
contrived for the unprocessed goods
of our food factories:

sows gainfully broad
on growth promotants and the turkeys bred
to be so self-weighted they lose not only flight
but upright carriage; think of crated chicks
in whole lives never touching ground,
calves slotted for months in stalls
too strait for turning round ...

How did we conceive
such mercy-stripped economies, save
by overhead example?
                    —a heartlessness born
in the sun's burning, here on islands like
    outgrown root-cramped pots, where survival's
    a business of waxing large enough
        to asphyxiate your rivals.

This is the land of seeds
sized like skulls, and thick-staggered palisades
behind which trunks lie mummied in a wrap of vines,
    and musks humming like corpses in the cooling
        breezes when, unconvincingly
        as ever, the sun again rinses
            bloody hands in the sea.

II. Very Tricky

Dusk and a substituting moon
its modest self upraising
from the companionable depths
and always the identical
illusion or insight:
same queer moment when
all but clear of the horizon
it seems to hesitate
palpate and finally abandon
the finish of geometry
the autonomy of the circle:
seems at the end to
bend to warp and in the attempt
not to be parted
with the sea-tied earth
to take on the susceptible
membranous elasticities
of a working heart

III. Very Still

Tonight the moon has set
its blueprints down upon the very site
long slated for construction.
                  If the belltower of
the island's topmost palm hasn't yet sounded,
    all is poised for the drawn-out flash,
    the bulldozing flame meant to raze
        the slopes to root and ash.

When the volcanic cone,
stripped to stone, echoes the moonlight, then can
assembly start in earnest: here ascend the airy
    atria, the salons and brilliant ballrooms,
    tiered terraces and concert halls,
    spiral staircases strung like grape-
        clusters to inner walls . . .

The dead alone shall slip
along its corridors of doors, sleep
alone through the dead hours of night when nothing stirs.
    Only the stars can tell them when to start
    their lengthy reclamation: spilling
    the clocks' workings, blanching the mirrors,
        chipping the friezes, milling

a fine dust-snow upon
marquetry, vitrine, mullioned windowpane,
weaving a web of cracks to bind ceiling to floor—
in sum, readying everything once more
for that hot sea of greenery
which, in one unretreating wave,
buries all utterly.

III   MEN AND MEN

AN OLD HUNTER

Up at four
and proud to make no delay; as the car
comes sliding up the drive, headlights dimmed,
he's slipping out the door.

At first he's
a little edgy, seeing they're all—
the other three—some thirty years his junior,
but soon a companionable ease

settles in,
with talk of the Lions (another loss),
a stolen lawnmower, someone's vanished girl,
and a few nips of gin.

It's not long before
he knows they *like* him—listening with clear
interest to his one short, pointed, wary
anecdote about the War.

And all the while
heading North, toward cleaner air, and trees
as if cleaner too—the shadowed oaks
lightening, mile by mile,

into birches bright
as lightning strokes. It looks like rain . . .
And it turns out every tree they pass,
and each small-town traffic light,

barn and billboard
and shaggy, disused railroad track,
all the clipped fields and the tall powerlines
steadily propel him toward

a naked, mud-brown
thicket beside a long low lake,
there to huddle with his rifle, and to wait,
as a fine rain comes down.

Oh, just to shake
the *chill* from his bones—but it's lodged so deep
even the bourbon in his flask can hardly
nudge it—and his knees ache,

and his shoulders ache,
and it's almost as if nothing will happen, ever
again, except the cold rain go on shivering
the dead surface of the lake.

*

So he slogs his way
out through the mud and back to the cabin,
hoping against hope he won't be the first of the group
to have called it a day—

which he is.
To make himself useful, he builds a big
fire that will welcome the others, and so they'll know
this little break of his

was meant to be brief,
he doesn't remove his hat or his coat
before drawing a folding chair up to the blaze.
But what a relief,

Lord knows, to feel
the heat go stealing through his calves!
He lets his eyes close, and though he doesn't sleep,
his glowing lids reveal

room upon room
of ideal gold, walls gold, and floors gold,
and each room warmer than the next, as if
in time he must come to some—

He's not asleep,
but when a log, hissing like a snake,
snaps with a resounding bang, his eyes spring open,
his old hands leap:

for a moment all un-
certain if this blast sent booming,
booming across the lake, comes from his own
or someone else's gun.

He taught *astronomy,*
And when I, five or six or so,
Blinked blindly at the word, "The stars," he added.
"I teach about the stars." The room, too, was dim,
The sun faded. And did I know
My *constellations?* Again he'd lit no light,
And yet my mute-kid's shrugged denial seemed
To nudge him with delight . . .
Even then, of course, it wasn't as if
My firmament had no features, was unclaimed—
Only that its rough, cohering puzzlings
Hadn't yet been named.

And that was his to do.
So Uncle Magnus, wheezing with
The emphysema that soon would bury him,
Took from the mantel a jam jar of pennies
And, star by star and myth by myth,
Richly laid out upon the threadbare
Rug a copper cosmos—dragon, horse, hunter,
Father and baby bear . . .
The heavens constructed, he then removed
Their capstone, handed it to me, said,
"Here's the North Star, this one's Polaris,"
Which I pocketed.

Still coruscating: this steel fantasy
    Outfitted for a king.
The whole astounding construct (fusing the hardware
    Of a streamlined technology
        With vines, urns, cherubs, and a matching
    Pair of full-bodied maidens, shoulders bare)
        Is sheathed in silver. The discs are mica,
    And the lens cases are of ivory.

Long years of hard-put labor clearly went
    Into its fashioning,
Whose craftsmanship in every dovetailed twist and turn
    (Screws cut to fifty threads an inch!) seems bent
        On making the case for everything
    We need being right before our eyes—each dawn
        The earth unveiling bounties such
    As ought to leave the hungriest soul content.

Yet it seems inwardness is in our blood:
    The deep-drawn urge to prise
Open the prism cells of a pared nail, to tear
    Tears apart, split hairs, follow that male flood
        Whose currents launch both the sunrise
    Duelist and the mooning sonneteer
        Down to its pools of frenzied tadpoles
    Blindly aswarm within a warm white mud.

Or turning back rather than down and in,
    Stooping—through time—to peer
At those two half-draped women whose plump arms enfold
    The slender body-tube that holds the twin
        Convex lenses, we might find here
    Poignantly quaint vestiges of that old
        Irretrievable marriage of
    Science and Art . . . although perhaps within

    The all-embracing sight of monarchy
        What principally was found
Were vindications of a root ancestral sense
    Of the demesne's extensibility
        Beyond the narrow mete and bound
    Of the surveyor's grounded measurements—
        Always the kingdom deeper, richer
    Than any bare, unprivileged eye could see.

BLESSING FOR MALCOLM LOWRY

His was a discriminating taste for error.
He once pinned a sharp little poem
on a printer's lapse—*tavern* appearing for
cavern—and in fact from the cavernous rear
of a bar one night I heard a rounded voice,
ripe with top-heavy certitude, pronounce,
"Life's a process of rile and terror"—
which too no doubt would've appealed to him.

This morning, early, I typed *damn* for *dawn*
and thought of him mumbling home, stumbling, cold,
daybreak, heartbreak, words in the head a flow
too full to follow, vows of a better life somehow
turned bitter: bitter laughter . . . A new leaf? The old
relief—and another damn day done in before the dawn.

IN THE WALL

I. A Near Miss

You stepped from the bookstore today
Into a mess of mist and rain, and I,
Driving past, catching sight of a long gray
Shape in the doorway, took you for another.
Not till you swung your big-jawed head at me,
    Features a blind scowl, did I see
That here was someone who'd once served as my
Soul-mate and confidant and now was neither.

Teacher, student, we learn by doing—
Or, in the case of one apprenticed to
The art of treachery, we learn by screwing
Our colleague and our neighbor, friend and spouse.
It's termite's labor—dark, clandestine, slow,
    No thanks and not a thing to show
For it until a thunderclapping breakthrough
Succeeds at last in bringing down the house.

Friend bloodies friend—what else is new?
Kindness is something most of us resent
And I (I can truly say) was kind to you.
You called me once—remember?—a life-saver.
Well, have you heard the one about the prof
    Whose trusted colleague knocks him off?
Funny (he thinks, as the blade goes in), I don't
Recall now ever doing *him* a favor . . .

II. Direct Hit

It rained as well—a warmer, tropical
Rain—on the morning when a thin myopic
Young man, bright and grim, brave and terrified,
Seated in an amphibious landing craft,
Squinted out at a green palm-crested atoll.
He looked in vain for a tell-tale glint, but not
Even the most sharp-sighted among his fellows
Could penetrate that ropey undergrowth.
(And now you see I have grown serious,
For niched within that emerald wall, well hidden,
With sights and guns, grenades and bunkers, waited
The enemy.) It was a sunless dawn.
They hit the beach. The young man—a boy, really—
Made it some twenty steps when he went (*Christ!*)
Down face flat to the sand. He'd lost his glasses,
Which was no loss, for he'd been knocked unconscious.
He was bleeding fast, the right half of his chest
Ripped open, which scarcely mattered either,
For ample wisdom had it that a man
Stranded there, on an open, shell-ripped beach,
Had only a few minutes anyway.

And that was all—it was a life—except
That now somebody shoulders him up and—
Two trunks, one pair of legs—plunges him onward,
Through the exploding air, into the leaves'

Shelter. His savior? No one he'd have known
Even if he'd been conscious. You might say
It was a uniform acknowledging
A uniform; or just a man, a man.

Now that's a gesture—slinging the limp body
Over your back while saying, Screw the danger,
Screw the damned snipers' rifles—I'm unable
To regard purely as a metaphor.
The wounded boy? My father,
                                              and the tale
Of his near-death was one he'd offer up
Every few years, and always with a sort
Of abashed incredulity, as if
Not quite able to say, *But don't you get it?*
It's not just me, it's the whole family,
All of us owe our presence to a stranger.

(All right, you might point out he bled to death
Anyway—but that day was still some forty
Years on, draining away inside himself
The morning a sort of bomb went off in his
Esophagus; and there was time enough,
Between the initial shelling and the next,
For such minor surmountings (the car at last
Paid off, the storms installed) and piquant joys
(Arriving home at dusk, a bag of doughnuts
Under your arm, or, wielding a breadknife

71

Your four-year-old insists you carry, heading
Down to the cellar, to prove how the bear
he'd dreamed of isn't there) as constitute
A life; and time enough to pass along
To each of his four sons the trailings of
An incredulity that was, for all
His bluffness, gentle—his a voice that seemed
To wish to say, The only feasible
Outlook on our existence is to be,
My sons, both awe-struck and unsentimental.)

III. Hit and Miss

Do I profane one of the dead
By drafting him, fresh in his war-wounds, merely
To chastise you? I'd like to think, instead,
He would be pleased to see me draw connections
Between the ambush laid with handshake and grin
  And those whose guns are genuine,
But if I kid myself, no matter; clearly,
The dead will survive even my resurrections.

What had been clever now looks cunning,
And what looked playful now's a killer's game.
Last week, for three nights running I was running—
Kept dreaming you pursued me with a knife.
I'd wake soaked through, but it was only sweat;
  I was untouched—unharmed—and yet
Each time I'd rise and rinse off all the same,
As though it *had* been blood. Here too's a life,

And rage is sweet to someone kept
A long time in the dark. Its flames begin
To rip a passage through the mist. You stepped
Out in the rain, I took you for another . . .
How fitting, that—the truth is I'd been wrong
  About your motives all along,
And more than just mistaken: taken in.
  Truth was, I took you for my brother.

Somehow having become someone who sets aside
a daily block of time in order to review
his list of grievances, you find yourself allied
with the gray, tireless woman in the stained blue
housedress who, most dawns, breakfasting on serial
cigarettes and black coffee, calmly reprimands
her late husband, point by point to the point where all
defenses crumble and he must throw up his hands;
and allied with the man who won't believe his brother
(my brother!) swindled him out of the family
business and so, each evening, hopeful with a numb
good faith, takes up the documents for yet another
trek down that paper trail which, inescapably,
deposits him before the same dumfounding sum . . .

When does it end?
When will the wounded heart,
that half-wit, comprehend the lesson which,
were it a dog or raccoon, only as smart
as the mice in the basement, it would have mastered
long since: there's no living on poison. When
perceive the only way to even a score
is to lose track of it, and no one-
sided argument was ever won?
Damn it, damn *you,* and how many months will have passed,
how many colossal cloud-shows brilliantly
fold up outside your window, before, like
them, like-minded, like-mindless, you learn at last
to turn a fresh configuration to the sun?

On the cold battlefield
in the mists before sunrise
they run through a series
of feints and forays,
the old pair of adversaries:
blue sky-patches advancing
as the gray shadow-shapes fold
into copse and fence row and back road . . .
It's the oldest tale
in the world: no convincing
some two to call a halt until
their shades of difference disappear
in the uncontainable outpour
of another spill of red.

SOMETHING OLD, SOMETHING NEW

We lived back then a quarter mile or so
from the Detroit Zoo and hot, airless nights
you might hear one of the big cats
calling. In lawn chairs on the patio
my Dad and I were sipping cans of Schlitz
(that was the first summer I'd been allowed
to drink with him), when through the darkness slid
a rumble—big, big as heat lightning. "It's
a lion," I say, and he says, just as if
it follows, "Uncle Teddy." "Mm?" "I guess
I'm thinking how in every person's life,
even the most ordinary man's,
there's one moment, maybe, something immense
stares him squarely in the face."

What surfaced was a small, a plump kind face.
Freckly red hands. A voice, plodding and clear,
that was a shoo-in for the rare
ritual of any family grace.
And big thick glasses with black frames. He once
gave me a gift: a measuring tape. It said,
"Grow a future," on one side,
on the other, "Time will toll." He sold insurance.
And had a *story*. At twenty-two he married
a perfect twin, the Doris feature of
a Doris/Doreen double bill,
and some three decades later, having buried . . .
But even now, the tale's my father's still,
the lions roar, once more he is alive.

"The phrase *company man* is one you never
hear except in ridicule
but that was Ted and Ted was no one's fool.
He was a joiner, who stepped up wherever
the magic words *We need a volunteer*
were spoken. Elks, Scouts, town fairs, bingo nights—
enough to drive a normal person nuts,
but that's I guess what made Teddy so dear
to everyone—his Let me play the cog
on someone else's wheel . . . Once, looking through
some family albums, hey, it all comes clear
to me: in *every* shot Ted's managed to
half-hide his face—bury an eye or ear
behind some deaf aunt, baby, even a dog.

"I know you know much of this but I'll tell
you anyway, is that all right?"
"Sure." "Going anywhere?" "No—not tonight."
"Where to start, then? His first wife? Doris? Well—
she was a looker. God he was so *proud*
of her! In time she had to make a rule
he couldn't buy her one more fur or jewel
or dress without her say-so first. Now, good
child of the Midwest that she was
she'd never seen the sea, and so he flew
her and the kids down to Cape Hatteras
and don't you know the very first day out
she's swept up in an undertow. She's through.
But he's got two small girls to think about.

"Sometimes the thought must have entered his brain
he'd married the wrong twin . . . But there was no
going back now, Doreen was taken now,
and Ted was desperate, which may help explain
why he married Aunt Adelle,
who stayed I don't know—two years? three?—and when
she left complained he'd been 'too nice' . . . Back then
it seemed to me almost unnatural
that any woman could just up and run
out on those kids who'd already lost one
Mom as it was; with time, though, it gets harder
to condemn anyone for anything.
She was a kid herself I suppose. Florida.
That's where she went. With some 'pool vacuum king.'

"Bride number three was Patsy, a rock-steady
Catholic girl. Mom used to call her plump
but that was kindness—better she'd said 'blimp':
in time, Patsy became *huge* . . . One day Teddy
admits the woman has now topped the three-
fifty-pound mark, which means—I figure out—
if down on one end of a scale you put
poor Pats, and on the other Mom and me
and you and Jumps and the pet mice,
she's still got thirty pounds on us.
But old Ted never turned a hair.
Maybe her weight comforted him, was seen
as more insurance for the insurance man?
Meant *this* one wasn't going anywhere?

"But go she did, where we must one and all . . .
One day, while loaded down with packages,
poor Pats—that packhorse of a woman—has
a heart attack in some damned mall
and I pray God when my time's up I won't
be standing in the checkout line at Sears . . .
We had a neighbor, Dick Storr (this was years
before you came along), who upped and went
in the world's most humiliating way.
Sweet guy, sold shoes, always wore a blue suit,
and *he* died, quiet, upright in his seat
in what we used to call the burlies. Look,
I don't suppose—" "Burlesque house . . ." "Hey,
don't tell me you've—" "No no. I've just heard talk."

"Dick Storr—hell, why'm I telling *this* to you?
But now that I've begun, I'd better add
that just the thought of Dick there, flat out dead
but eyes wide open, and the girl going through
the routine motions of her dance—
give 'em a bump, a leer, a wink,
a little shiver . . . Life, I sometimes think,
is crueler than we are, if that makes sense."
He stopped. Crickets were making sounds the stars
might make if they weren't mute. "And Teddy? Years
went by. He was alone. Then one day Jerry,
Doreen's husband, gets hit by a—I swear—a
Mack truck. On Seven Mile. Which leaves the twin
of Ted's beloved Doris free. Imagine.

"It's all so proper: whole thing's oh so slow.
Not to fool anybody, but because
that's just the way Ted always was—
courtly. He courts her just as though
he hadn't known her more than half his life,
beginning back when she was just a kid
in pigtails (not to mention having had
her carbon copy as his wife).
One time your Mom and I promised to go
to Cleveland with them—you were going to stay
with Grams—but when your Mom's laid low
with hepatitis what does Teddy say?
Grandly declares the trip 'will be postponed.'
Wouldn't be proper—mm?—to go unchaperoned.

"But in the end maybe we all arrive
where properness, correctness—oh hell, what's
the word I'm after? *You're* the writer . . ." It's
a joke, but pride is in it—proud that I've
been named Junior Assistant Copy Chief
of the school paper. ". . . there's a moment where
such things give out. I'm speaking now of their
first time, the—their first night as man and wife.
That too comes back." His quiet voice
frays to a bare whisper. I hear him drink,
and swallow. "Time and time again. I think
that maybe this was Uncle Teddy's one
key moment, *this* was the one when
he met his own life face to face.

"I don't know what you know of—what you've done
about—I can't believe you want me poking
around your personal—" . . . If you were asking,
Father, whether your sixteen-year-old son,
head bobbing in a two-can sea of beer,
was still a virgin, let me now confess
that I was guilty of that innocence.
But if you meant did I see just how *queer*
your story was, that answer too was yes.
Like you, I might say *time and time again;*
by now, I can't begin to guess
how many times I've heard your voice that night,
assessing me. It looms as the one great
exchange of our lives, the night when

you struggled to protect me somehow
from the wide world, while seeking, in a fear-
sheared voice, to get me, man to man, to share
with you a mortal burden . . . Even now
I'd have you know (but you've gone underground,
and if you passed on in a hospital bed
rather than some "damned mall," still you are dead,
which seems a bitter deal all round)
you made your point: that evening, as the great
cats called for their walls to go smash,
that they might, tail-tufts lifted like a firebrand,
parade our streets, reclaim the night,
I caught—half admonition and half wish—
your lesson: *Men and women! There's no end,*

no end to what they'll do! To grasp
your twisted tale, your virgin son
had first to lighten his uncle one by one
of overcoat, suit coat, cufflinks, tie clasp,
necktie, suspenders, shirt, shoes, socks, and pants,
and underpants; next, strip shoes, hat, and what
was placed between, from Aunt Doreen; then set
them going in a dim unholy dance:
   Save for his watch and thick glasses, Ted stands
naked. The woman too. She's back—almost
come back to him, who lacks the ability
to move . . . *She* moves, moves toward him—and he? He
(his vast, lens-bloated eyes fixed on a ghost)
now fits a living woman to his hands.

CREST AND CARPET

I often picture it as a great cold
mountain—your death—as if you

selected it somehow, chose
your treeless summit from which to stare

down on us forever: the world's flat, there
in that vision I hold to, and yet goes

on unrolling beneath you, or being unrolled,
like a carpet, and each day's a new

turning, a further spreading out,
and I wonder of you on your mountain Just

what can it be like, how must
you be feeling, as you watch friends

and family busily go about
their ever more distant errands?

A NOTE ABOUT THE AUTHOR

Brad Leithauser was born in Detroit and graduated from Harvard College and Harvard Law School. He is the author of three other volumes of poetry (*Hundreds of Fireflies, Cats of the Temple,* and *The Mail from Anywhere*), four novels (*Equal Distance, Hence, Seaward,* and *The Friends of Freeland*), and a book of essays (*Penchants and Places*). He also edited *The Norton Book of Ghost Stories.* He is the recipient of many awards for his writing, including a Guggenheim Fellowship, an Ingram Merrill grant, and a MacArthur Fellowship. He recently served for a year as *Time* magazine's theater critic. He and his wife, the poet Mary Jo Salter, are the Emily Dickinson Lecturers in the Humanities at Mount Holyoke College. They live with their two daughters, Emily and Hilary, in South Hadley, Massachusetts.

A NOTE ON THE TYPE

The text of this book was set in a digitized version of Bembo, the well-known monotype face. The original cutting of Bembo was made by Francesco Griffo of Bologna only a few years after Columbus discovered America. It was named after Pietro Bembo, the celebrated Renaissance writer and humanist scholar who was made a cardinal and served as secretary to Pope Leo X. Sturdy, well-balanced, and finely proportioned, Bembo is a face of rare beauty. It is, at the same time, extremely legible in all of its sizes.

Composed by NK Graphics, Keene, New Hampshire

Printed at The Stinehour Press, Lunenburg, Vermont

Bound at The Book Press, Brattleboro, Vermont